Adding to 10

There are 10 cubes in each group.

How many are in each bag?

1

ı. 6 + 4 = 1 0

2

3

4

5

6

7

8

9

10

Write the missing numbers.

11 8 + 🌸 = 10

ıı. 8 + 2 = 1 0

12 6 + 🌸 = 10

13 9 + 🌸 = 10

14 5 + 🌸 = 10

15 2 + 🌸 = 10

16 7 + 🌸 = 10

17 1 + 🌸 = 10

18 3 + 🌸 = 10

19 4 + 🌸 = 10

20 10 + 🌸 = 10

Each screen had 20 monsters.

How many have been blasted?

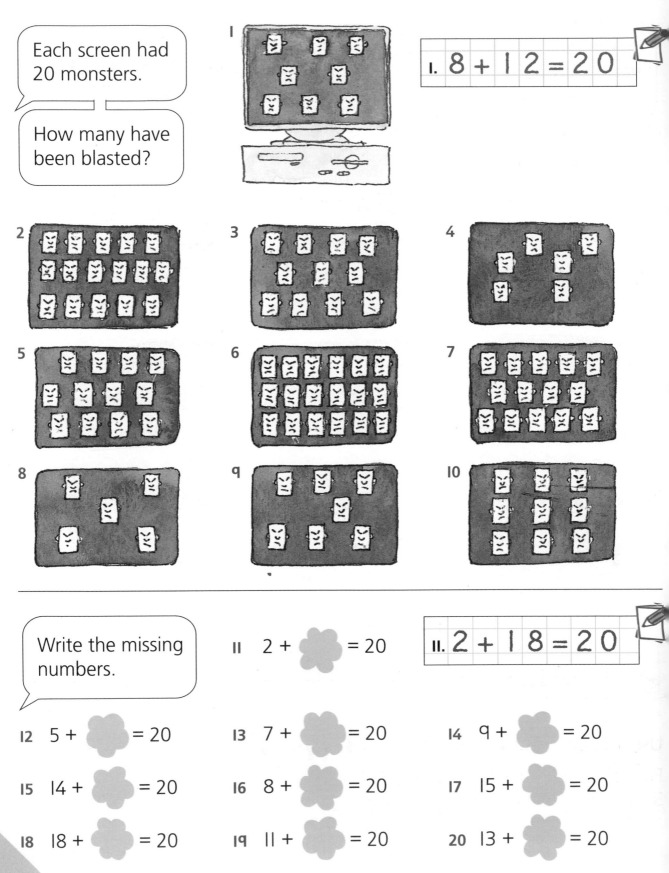

1. $8 + 12 = 20$

Write the missing numbers.

11   $2 + = 20$

11. $2 + 18 = 20$

12   $5 + = 20$

13   $7 + = 20$

14   $9 + = 20$

15   $14 + = 20$

16   $8 + = 20$

17   $15 + = 20$

18   $18 + = 20$

19   $11 + = 20$

20   $13 + = 20$

Adding to 20

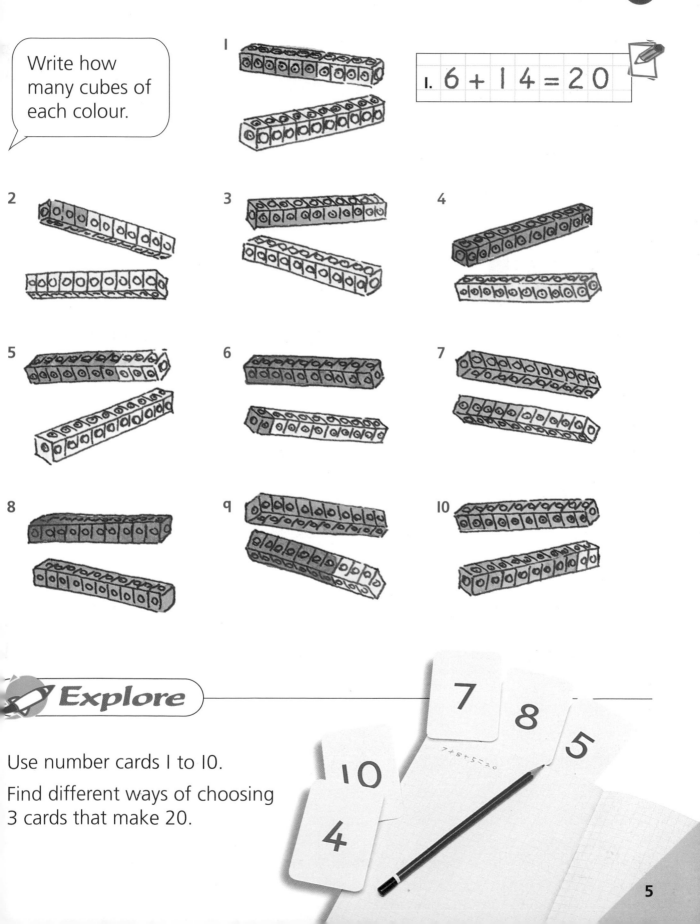

Write how many cubes of each colour.

1.

1. $6 + 14 = 20$

2

3

4

5

6

7

8

9

10

Explore

Use number cards 1 to 10.

Find different ways of choosing 3 cards that make 20.

7

8

5

10

$7 + 8 + 5 = 20$

4

Differences

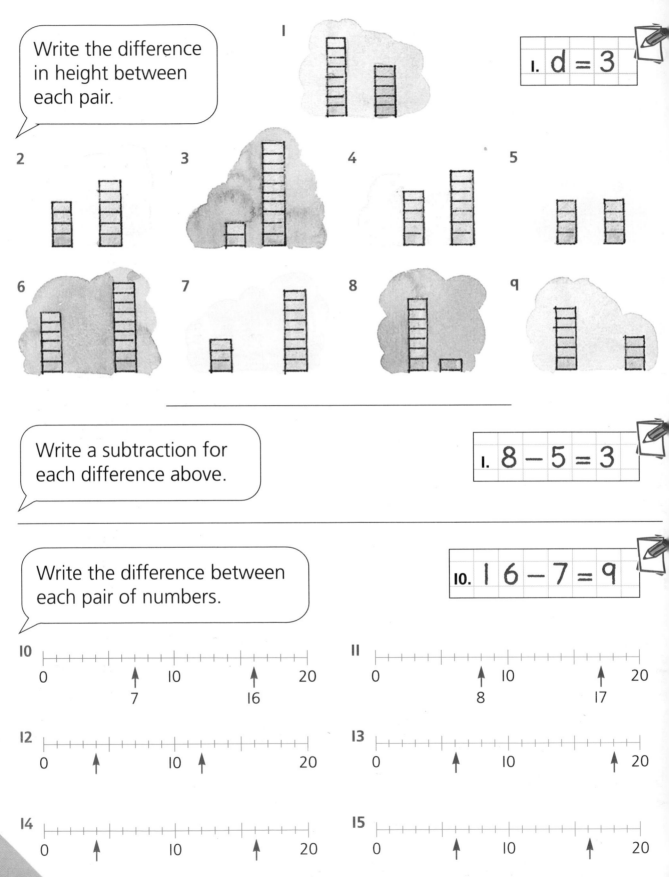

Write the difference in height between each pair.

I. $d = 3$

Write a subtraction for each difference above.

I. $8 - 5 = 3$

Write the difference between each pair of numbers.

IO. $16 - 7 = 9$

10 0   7   10   16   20

11 0   8   10   17   20

12 0   10   20

13 0   10   20

14 0   10   20

15 0   10   20

Differences

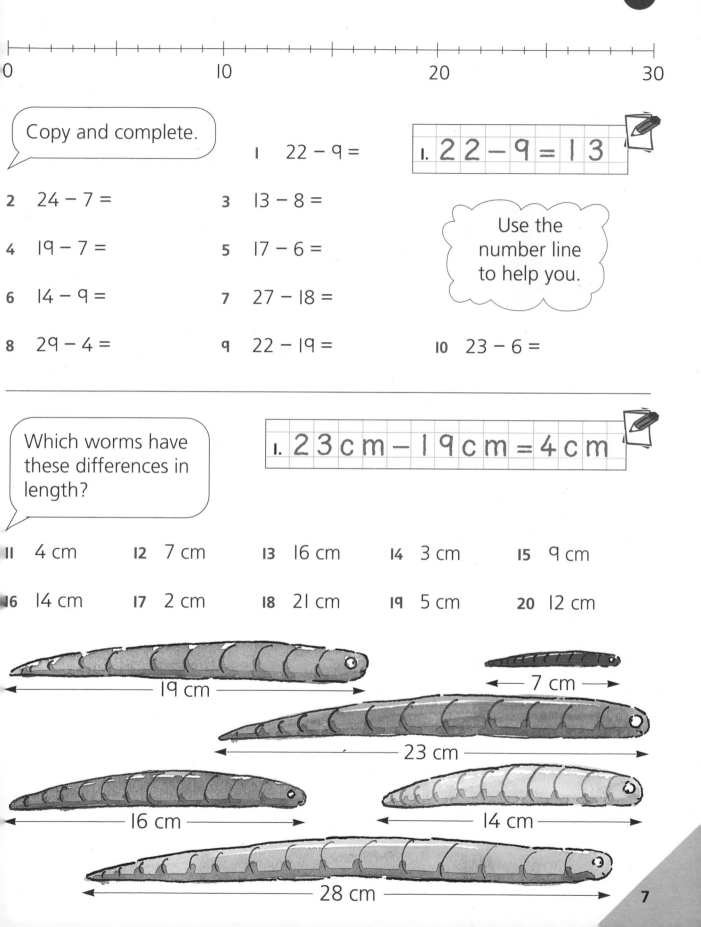

0   10   20   30

Copy and complete.

1   22 − 9 =

1. $22 - 9 = 13$

2   24 − 7 =   3   13 − 8 =

Use the number line to help you.

4   19 − 7 =   5   17 − 6 =

6   14 − 9 =   7   27 − 18 =

8   29 − 4 =   9   22 − 19 =   10   23 − 6 =

Which worms have these differences in length?

1. $23\,cm - 19\,cm = 4\,cm$

11   4 cm   12   7 cm   13   16 cm   14   3 cm   15   9 cm

16   14 cm   17   2 cm   18   21 cm   19   5 cm   20   12 cm

19 cm

7 cm

23 cm

16 cm

14 cm

28 cm

Differences

Write the difference between each pair.

1. 17p 26p   1. $26p - 17p = 9p$

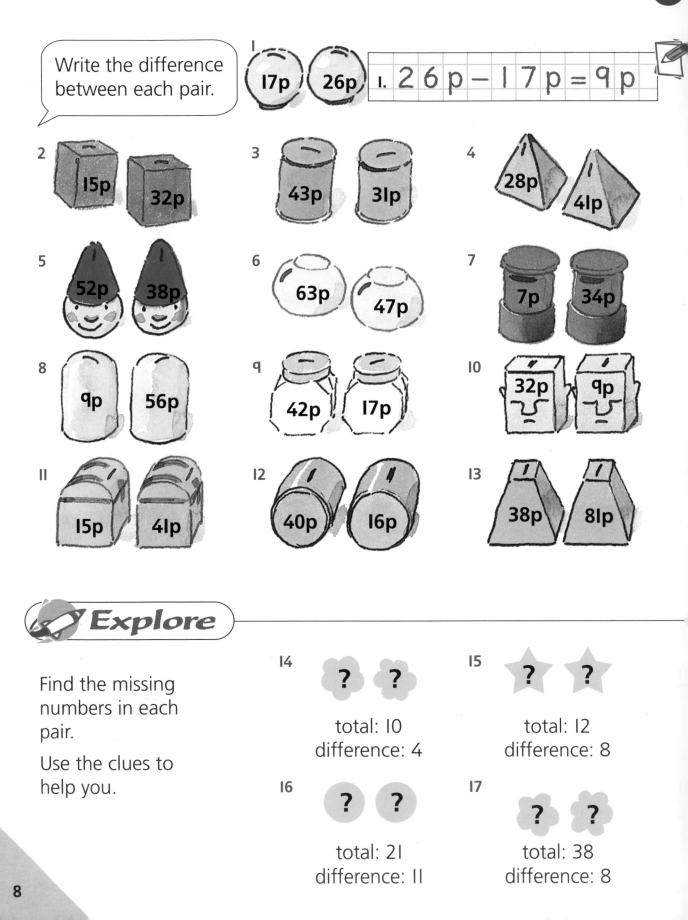

2. 15p 32p

3. 43p 31p

4. 28p 41p

5. 52p 38p

6. 63p 47p

7. 7p 34p

8. 9p 56p

9. 42p 17p

10. 32p 9p

11. 15p 41p

12. 40p 16p

13. 38p 81p

Explore

Find the missing numbers in each pair.

Use the clues to help you.

14. ? ?
total: 10
difference: 4

15. ? ?
total: 12
difference: 8

16. ? ?
total: 21
difference: 11

17. ? ?
total: 38
difference: 8

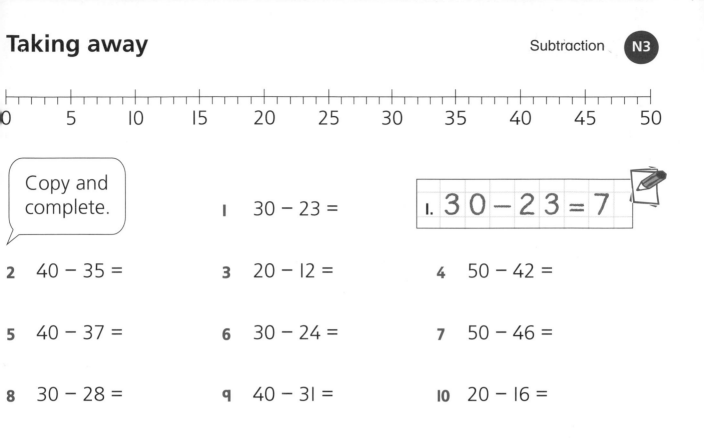

Copy and complete.

1 30 − 23 =

ı. 30 − 23 = 7

2 40 − 35 =

3 20 − 12 =

4 50 − 42 =

5 40 − 37 =

6 30 − 24 =

7 50 − 46 =

8 30 − 28 =

9 40 − 31 =

10 20 − 16 =

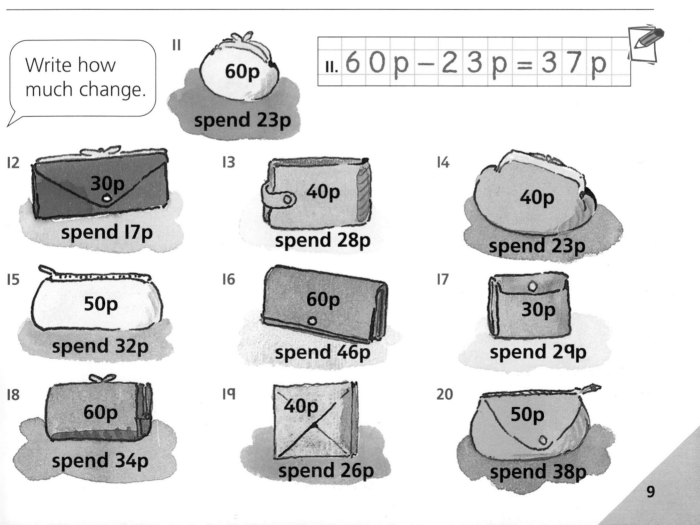

Write how much change.

11 60p

ıı. 60p − 23p = 37p

spend 23p

12 30p
spend 17p

13 40p
spend 28p

14 40p
spend 23p

15 50p
spend 32p

16 60p
spend 46p

17 30p
spend 29p

18 60p
spend 34p

19 40p
spend 26p

20 50p
spend 38p

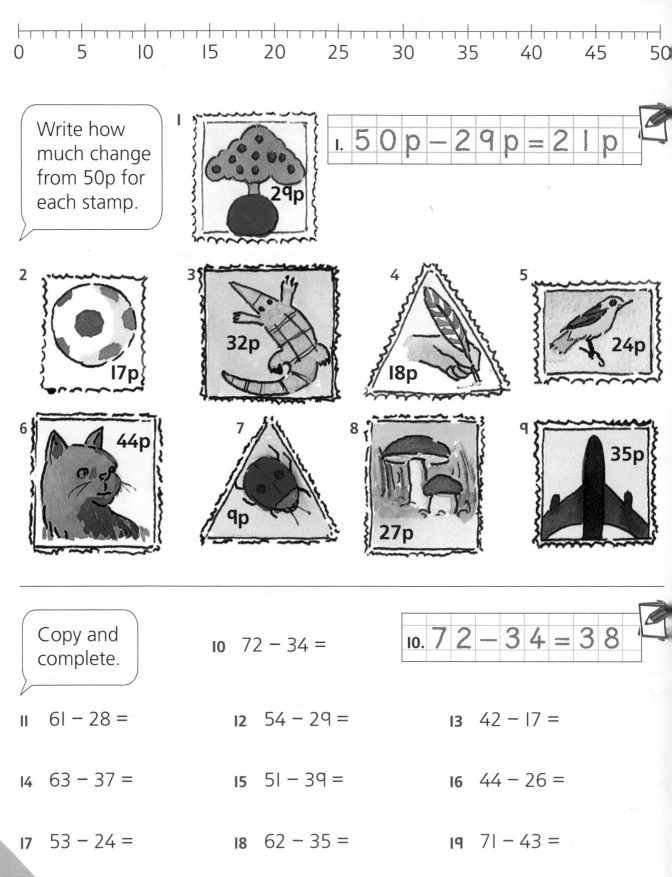

Write how much change from 50p for each stamp.

1. $50p - 29p = 21p$

1. 29p

2. 17p

3. 32p

4. 18p

5. 24p

6. 44p

7. 9p

8. 27p

9. 35p

Copy and complete.

10 $72 - 34 =$

10. $72 - 34 = 38$

11 $61 - 28 =$

12 $54 - 29 =$

13 $42 - 17 =$

14 $63 - 37 =$

15 $51 - 39 =$

16 $44 - 26 =$

17 $53 - 24 =$

18 $62 - 35 =$

19 $71 - 43 =$

Taking away

> The tower is 70 steps high.

> How many steps does each child go down to reach the bottom?

1. $70 - 24 = 46$

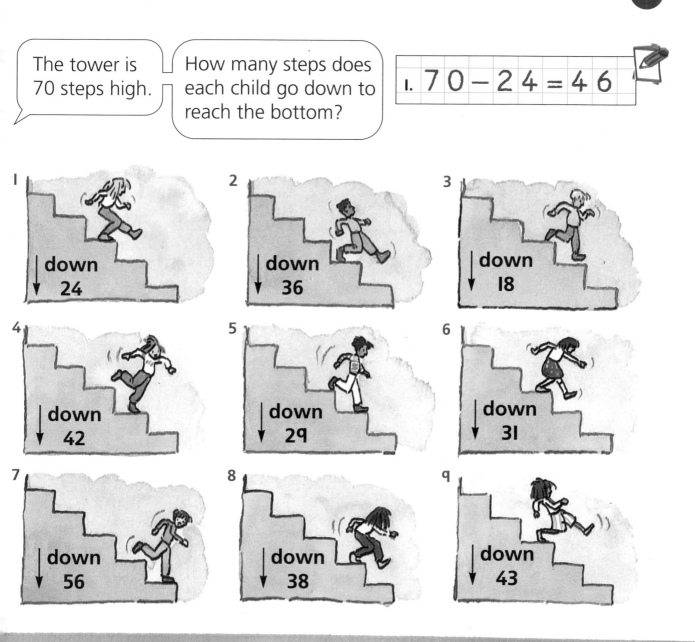

1. down 24
2. down 36
3. down 18
4. down 42
5. down 29
6. down 31
7. down 56
8. down 38
9. down 43

At Home

Imagine all television programmes were shown 19 minutes early.

Write the old and new times of your 3 favourite programmes.

Draw a picture to go with each.

11

Write the difference in price between each pair.

1. $38p - 25p = 13p$

1. 25p   38p

2. 47p   26p

3. 62p   49p

4. 83p   66p

5. 55p   39p

6. 70p   55p

7. 34p   18p

8. 41p   29p

9. 17p   25p

Explore

Measure the lengths of six long objects, in centimetres.

Write the differences in length between pairs.

table → 89 cm
shelf → 53 cm

89 cm − 53 cm = 36 cm

Multiplying

Write how many stickers in each set.

1.

1. $2 \times 4 = 8$

2 × 4 is two rows of four.

2

3

4

5

6

7

8

q

Draw sets of stickers to match these.

10 3×2

10.

11 2×5

12 4×3

13 1×6

14 6×4

15 3×6

16 4×2

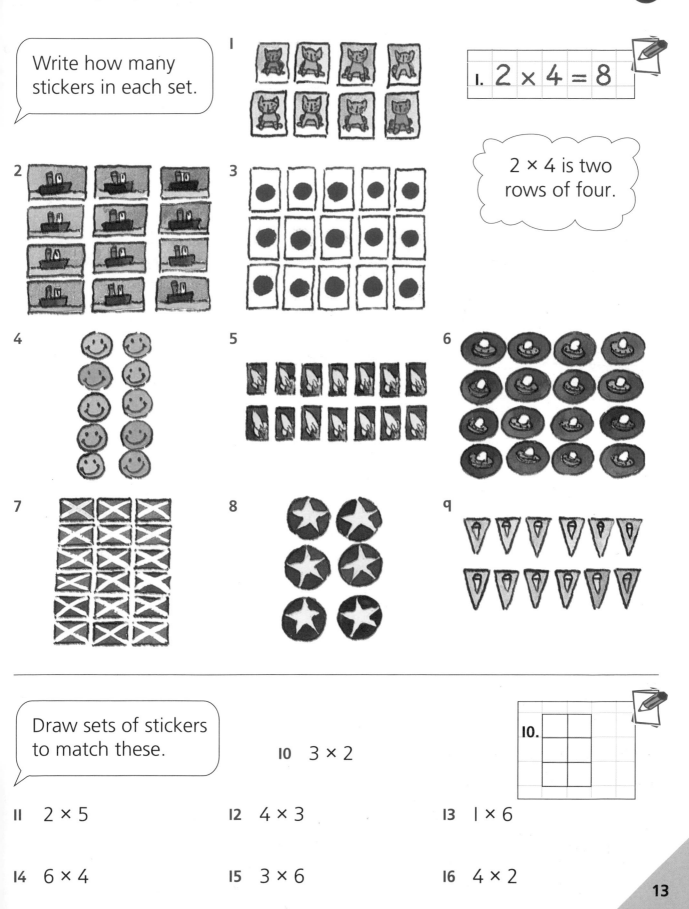

Multiplying

Write how many buns in each set.

1.

1. $2 \times 4 = 8$

2

3

4

Write multiplications to match.

5. $3 \times 2 = 2 \times 3$

5

6

7

8

9

10

11

12

13

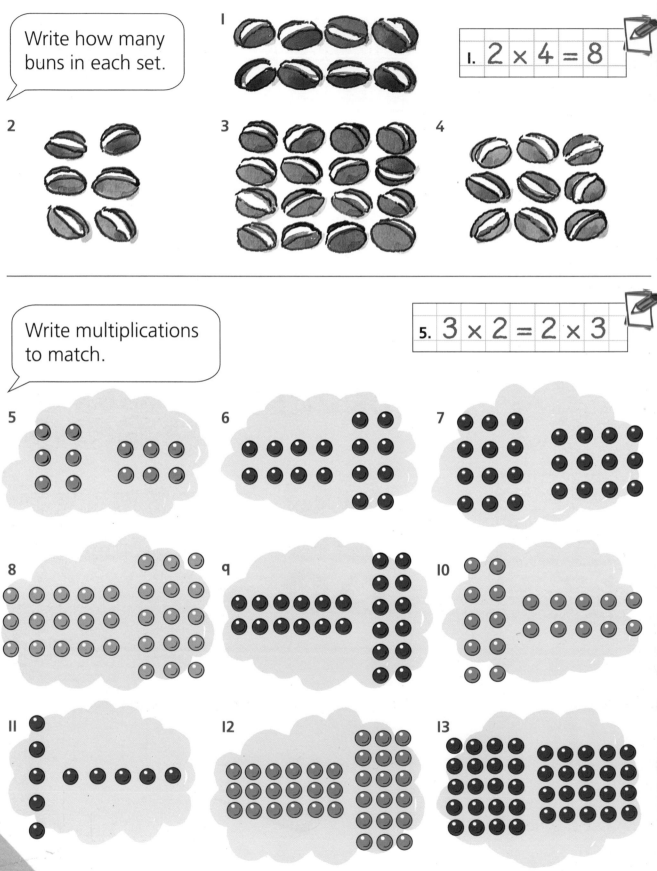

14

Multiplying

Write a multiplication for each grid.

1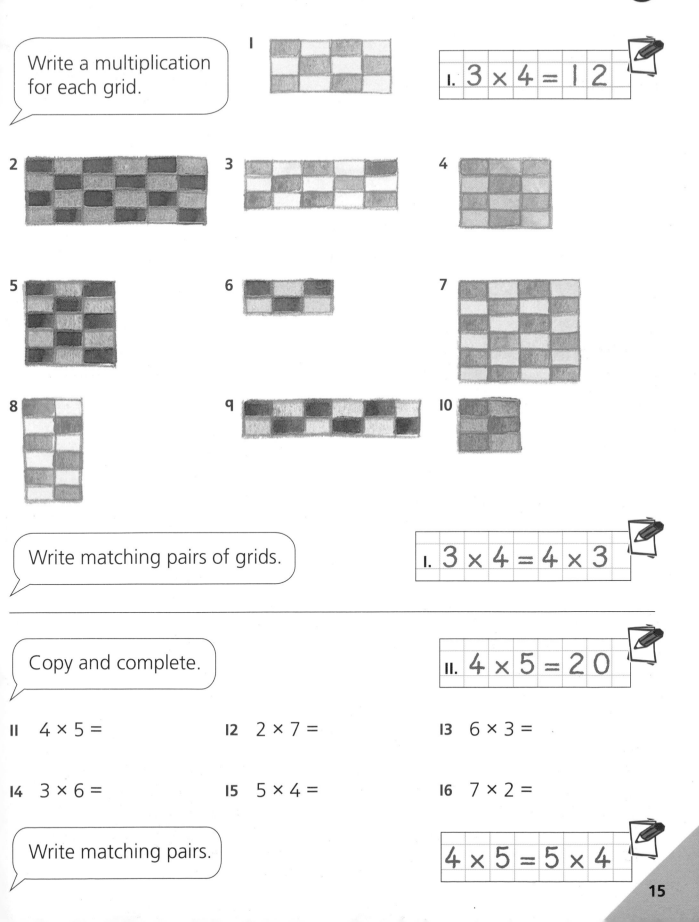

1. $3 \times 4 = 12$

2

3

4

5

6

7

8

9

10

Write matching pairs of grids.

1. $3 \times 4 = 4 \times 3$

Copy and complete.

II. $4 \times 5 = 20$

11 $4 \times 5 =$

12 $2 \times 7 =$

13 $6 \times 3 =$

14 $3 \times 6 =$

15 $5 \times 4 =$

16 $7 \times 2 =$

Write matching pairs.

$4 \times 5 = 5 \times 4$

Write pairs of children with the same number of stamps.

ı. Andy and Jan

$4 \times 3 = 3 \times 4$

Andy

Cody

Tom

Seema

Carla

Jill

David

Jan

Tim

Anil

Kate

Mike

Explore

Use squared paper.

These rectangles all have 8 squares.

How many different rectangles can you draw which all have 12 squares?

$1 \times 8 = 8$

$8 \times 1 = 8$

Multiplying

Copy and complete.

Write a matching multiplication.

1. $8 \times 2 = 16$

$2 \times 8 = 16$

1 $\times 2 = 16$

2 $3 \times = 12$

3 $\times 5 = 10$

4 $6 \times = 18$

5 $\times 10 = 30$

6 $\times 2 = 14$

7 $9 \times = 45$

8 $1 \times = 6$

9 $8 \times = 24$

10 $\times 7 = 28$

11 $\times 2 = 18$

12 $5 \times 4 = $

13 $4 \times = 32$

14 $\times 4 = 24$

15 $6 \times = 60$

Explore

How many multiplication pairs can you write with an answer of 24?

How many can you write with an answer of 18? Or of 60?

$6 \times 4 = 24$
$4 \times 6 = 24$

17

Double the number of cubes.

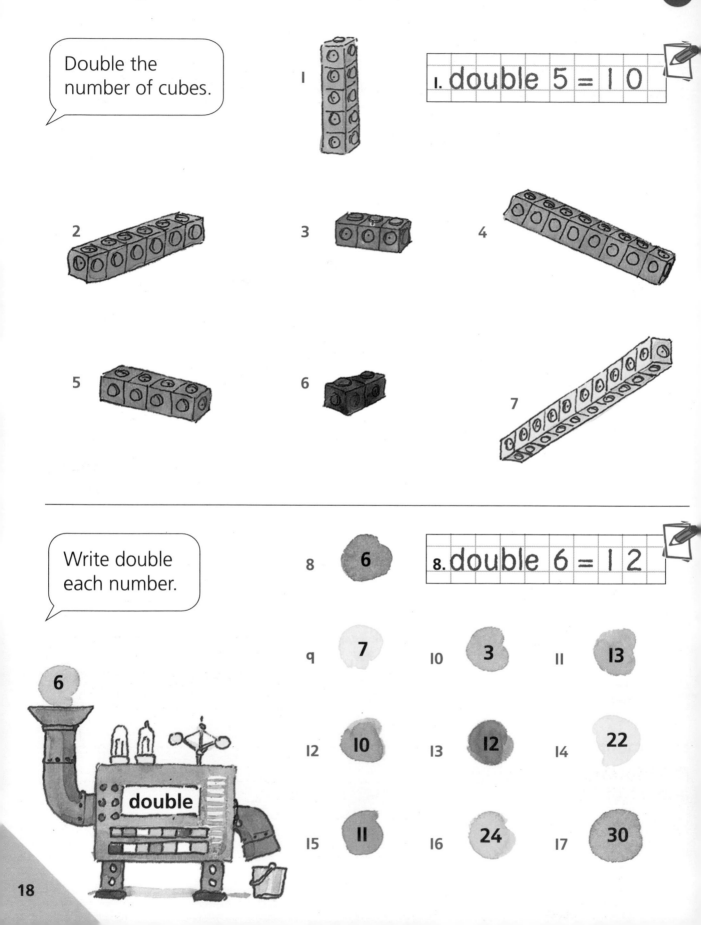

1 | 1. double 5 = 10

2

3

4

5

6

7

Write double each number.

8   6 | 8. double 6 = 12

double

9   7   10   3   11   13

6

12   10   13   12   14   22

15   11   16   24   17   30

18

Doubling

Write how much two of each costs.

1 Beans **23p**

1. double 2 3 p = 4 6 p

2 Flour **42p**

3 **31p** Cola

4 Crisps **18p**

5 **25p** Chocolate

6 **13p**

7 **35p**

8 Bread **47p**

9 Soup **28p**

Copy and complete the tables.

in	1 5	2 5		
double	3 0			

in	15	25	35	45	55	65	75	85
double								

in	20	30	40	50	60	70	80	90
double								

Doubling

Each child doubles the score.

Write the new scores.

1

Score 18

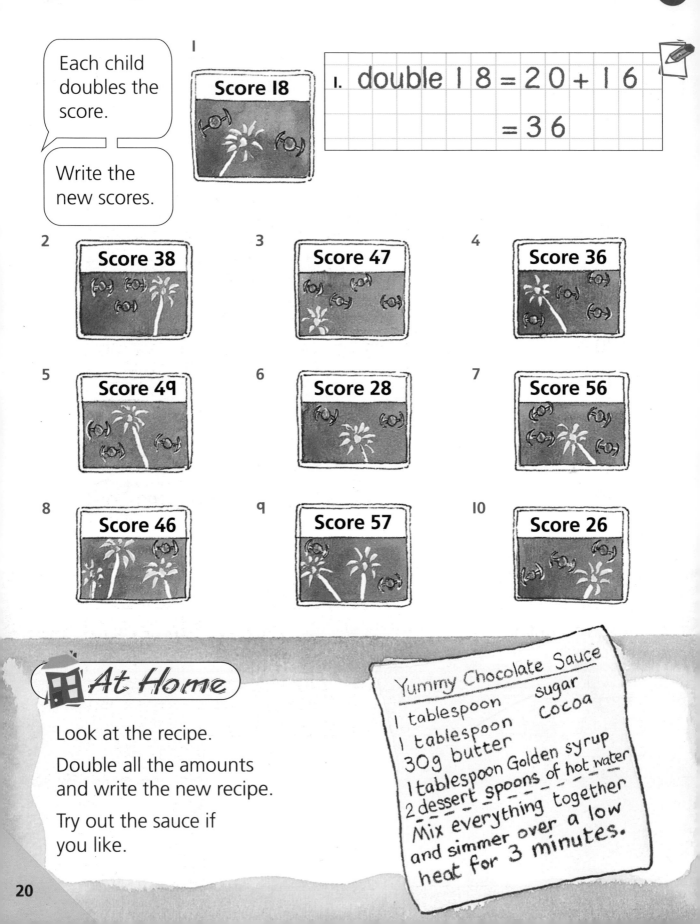

1. double 18 = 20 + 16
            = 36

2 Score 38

3 Score 47

4 Score 36

5 Score 49

6 Score 28

7 Score 56

8 Score 46

9 Score 57

10 Score 26

At Home

Look at the recipe.

Double all the amounts and write the new recipe.

Try out the sauce if you like.

Yummy Chocolate Sauce

1 tablespoon   sugar
1 tablespoon   cocoa
30g butter
1 tablespoon Golden syrup
2 dessert spoons of hot water

Mix everything together and simmer over a low heat for 3 minutes.

Adding tens

Add 10 to each spider number.

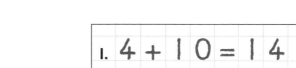

I. $4 + 10 = 14$

1   $4 + 10 =$

2   $17 + 10 =$

3   $23 + 10 =$

4   $38 + 10 =$

5   $45 + 10 =$

6   $52 + 10 =$

7   $66 + 10 =$

8   $79 + 10 =$

9   $81 + 10 =$

10   $94 + 10 =$

1	2	3	4	5	6	7	8	9	10
11	12	13	14	15	16	17	18	19	20
21	22	23	24	25	26	27	28	29	30
31	32	33	34	35	36	37	38	39	40
41	42	43	44	45	46	47	48	49	50
51	52	53	54	55	56	57	58	59	60
61	62	63	64	65	66	67	68	69	70
71	72	73	74	75	76	77	78	79	80
81	82	83	84	85	86	87	88	89	90
91	92	93	94	95	96	97	98	99	100

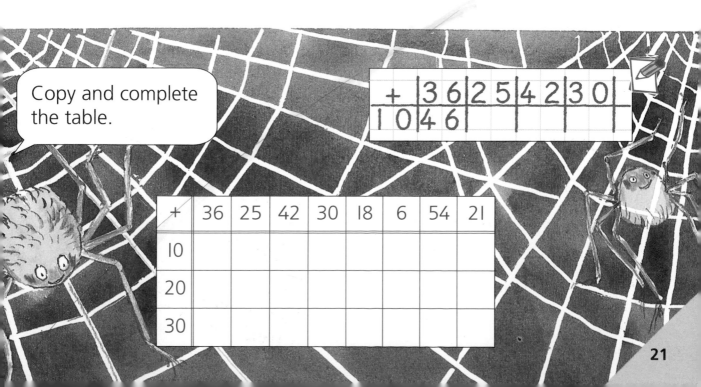

Copy and complete the table.

+	36	25	42	30				
10	46							

+	36	25	42	30	18	6	54	21
10								
20								
30								

Adding tens

> Choose 10 numbers from the grid.

> Add 20 to each.

1. $24 + 20 = 44$

1	2	3	4	5	6	7	8	9	10
11	12	13	14	15	16	17	18	19	20
21	22	23	24	25	26	27	28	29	30
31	32	33	34	35	36	37	38	39	40
41	42	43	44	45	46	47	48	49	50
51	52	53	54	55	56	57	58	59	60
61	62	63	64	65	66	67	68	69	70
71	72	73	74	75	76	77	78	79	80
81	82	83	84	85	86	87	88	89	90
91	92	93	94	95	96	97	98	99	100

> Copy and complete.

11 $46 + 20 =$

11. $46 + 20 = 66$

12 $64 + 30 =$

13 $27 + 40 =$

14 $ + 10 = 54$

15 $ + 20 = 75$

16 $39 + 20 =$

17 $42 + 30 =$

18 $16 + 40 =$

19 $34 + = 64$

20 $ + 20 = 99$

22

Adding

Add 30p to each bank.

1.
26p

I. $26p + 30p = 56p$

2. 32p

3. 44p

4. 56p

5. 25p

Copy and complete.

6. $46 + 24 = 70$

Use the number grid to help you.

6 $46 + 24 =$

7 $54 + 26 =$

8 $33 + 27 =$

9 $58 + 32 =$

10 $71 + 29 =$

11 $27 + 33 =$

12 $66 + 25 =$

13 $39 + 31 =$

14 $82 + 18 =$

15 $77 + 21 =$

1	2	3	4	5	6	7	8	9	10
11	12	13	14	15	16	17	18	19	20
21	22	23	24	25	26	27	28	29	30
31	32	33	34	35	36	37	38	39	40
41	42	43	44	45	46	47	48	49	50
51	52	53	54	55	56	57	58	59	60
61	62	63	64	65	66	67	68	69	70
71	72	73	74	75	76	77	78	79	80
81	82	83	84	85	86	87	88	89	90
91	92	93	94	95	96	97	98	99	100

Adding

 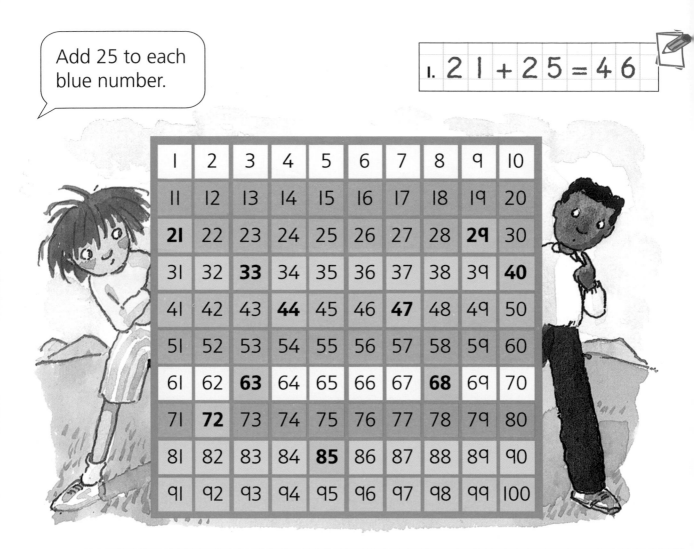

Add 25 to each blue number.

I. $21 + 25 = 46$

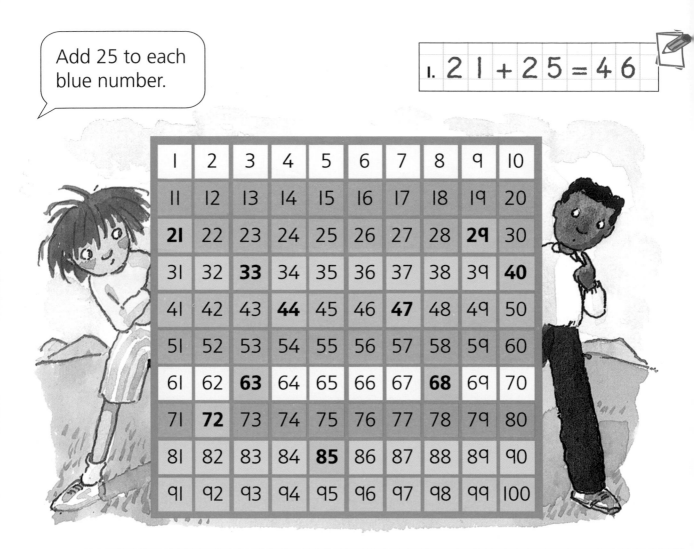

Each flower grows 18 cm. Write the new heights.

II. $27\,cm + 18\,cm = 45\,cm$

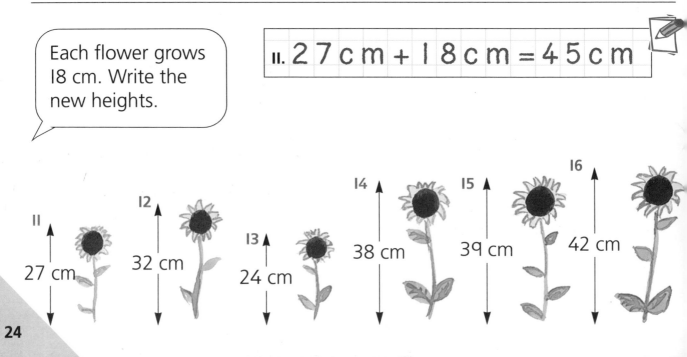

11. 27 cm 12. 32 cm 13. 24 cm 14. 38 cm 15. 39 cm 16. 42 cm

24

Adding

Which page is 17 more?

1.
$$36 + 17 = 53$$

(36)

2. (57)

3. (66)

4. (41)

5. (28)

6. (74)

7. (17)

Copy and complete.

8   $38 + 26 =$

8.
$$38 + 26 = 64$$

9   $57 + 18 =$

10   $64 + 27 =$

11   $48 + 27 =$

12   $56 + 25 =$

13   $75 + 36 =$

14   $59 + 23 =$

Explore

Write numbers in the spaces to make the addition correct.

Use cards to help you.

How many ways can you find?

$$1\square + \square\square = 1\square 1$$

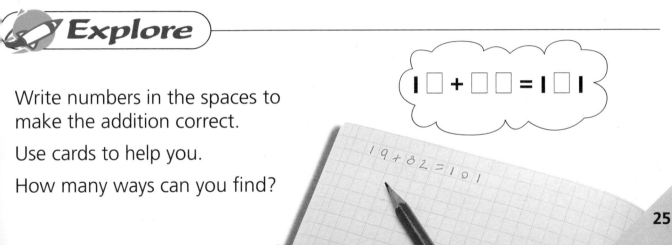

$19 + 82 = 101$

Adding

Write how much money in total.

I. 4 4 p + 3 6 p = 8 0 p

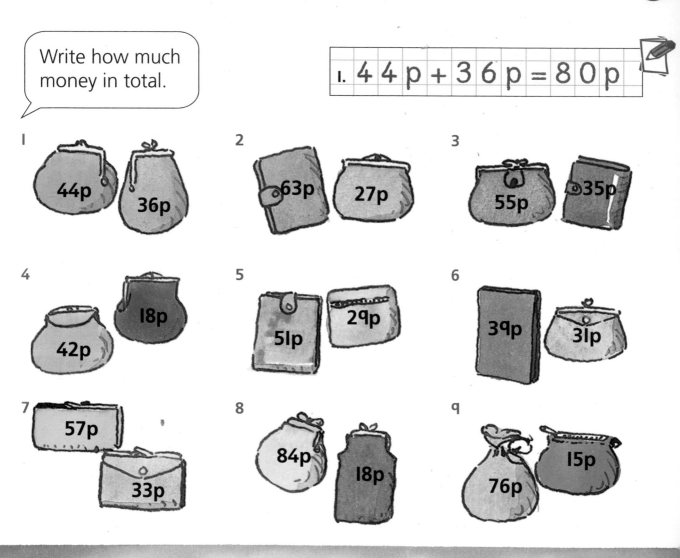

1. 44p 36p
2. 63p 27p
3. 55p 35p
4. 42p 18p
5. 51p 29p
6. 39p 31p
7. 57p 33p
8. 84p 18p
9. 76p 15p

At Home

A game for 2 players.

Make ten cards numbered 0 to 9. Shuffle them and take four each.

Make two 2-digit numbers and add them.

The player with the lowest score takes a counter. Play again.

Who is the first to collect five counters?

18 + 34 = 52

Adding

Copy and complete.

Look for tens.

1
```
  H  T  U
     3  5
     4  6
+    7  5
_____
```

```
   H T U
1.   3 5
     4 6
+    7 5
_____
   1 5 6
     1
```

2
```
  H  T  U
     2  1
     8  6
+    1  9
_____
```

3
```
  H  T  U
     4  4
     2  7
+    6  6
_____
```

4
```
  H  T  U
     3  2
     7  6
+    2  8
_____
```

5
```
  H  T  U
     4  3
     2  7
+    6  5
_____
```

6
```
  H  T  U
     2  5
     4  3
+    8  5
_____
```

7
```
  H  T  U
     6  4
     3  1
+    4  6
_____
```

8
```
  H  T  U
     6  3
     2  7
+    4  1
_____
```

9
```
  H  T  U
     1  9
     2  1
+    8  3
_____
```

Choose 3 bags. Find the total weight.

Do this 5 times.

25 kg   46 kg   52 kg   28 kg   34 kg

```
   H T U
     2 5
     4 6
+    3 4
_____
   1 0 5 kg
     1
```

Adding

Copy and complete.

Add 9 by adding 10 and taking 1 away.

1.
```
    H  T  U
       2  7
       3  6
+      1  9
-----------
```

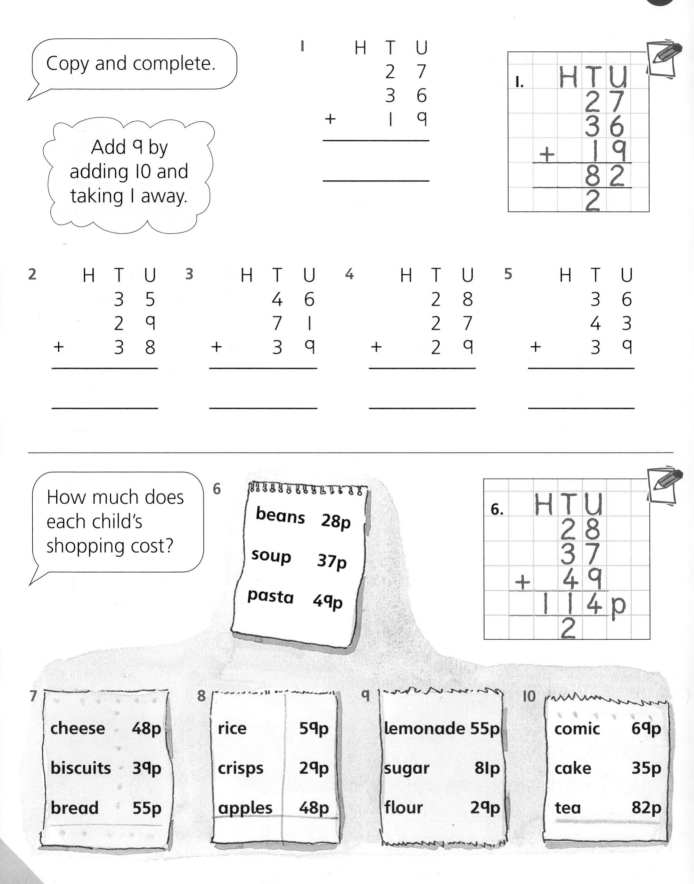

1.
```
   H  T  U
      2  7
      3  6
+     1  9
----------
      8  2
      2
```

2.
```
   H  T  U
      3  5
      2  9
+     3  8
----------
```

3.
```
   H  T  U
      4  6
      7  1
+     3  9
----------
```

4.
```
   H  T  U
      2  8
      2  7
+     2  9
----------
```

5.
```
   H  T  U
      3  6
      4  3
+     3  9
----------
```

How much does each child's shopping cost?

6.

beans   28p

soup   37p

pasta   49p

6.
```
   H  T  U
      2  8
      3  7
+     4  9
----------
   1  1  4 p
      2
```

7.
cheese   48p

biscuits   39p

bread   55p

8.
rice   59p

crisps   29p

apples   48p

9.
lemonade 55p

sugar   81p

flour   29p

10.
comic   69p

cake   35p

tea   82p

Adding

> Copy and complete.

> Look for tens.
> Add any nines.

1

```
      H  T  U
         2  4
         3  6
         1  9
   +     2  8
   _____
```

```
I.    H  T  U
         2  4
         3  6
         1  9
   +     2  8
   _____
      1  0  7
         2
```

2
```
   H  T  U
      3  4
      1  8
      2  9
+     2  2
_____
```

3
```
   H  T  U
      2  7
      3  3
      4  9
+     2  7
_____
```

4
```
   H  T  U
      3  6
      1  7
      3  4
+     2  9
_____
```

5
```
   H  T  U
      4  5
      3  9
      2  5
+     3  6
_____
```

6
```
   H  T  U
      2  6
      3  7
      4  9
+     4  4
_____
```

7
```
   H  T  U
      1  9
      4  6
      5  2
+     1  8
_____
```

8
```
   H  T  U
      2  7
      3  3
      4  9
+     4  0
_____
```

9
```
   H  T  U
      2  6
      2  7
      3  9
+     4  3
_____
```

Explore

Use number cards 1 to 8.

Make four 2-digit numbers and add them.

What are the largest and smallest totals you can make?

What other totals can you make?

```
   H  T  U
      1  3
      2  7
      5  4
+     8  6
_____
   1  8  0
      2
```

Adding

> Copy and complete.

1.
```
  H T U
    3 4
    6 7
    4 6
+   2 8
_____

_____
```

2.
```
  H T U
    2 9
    3 5
    4 6
+   7 2
_____

_____
```

3.
```
  H T U
    2 8
    3 6
    4 8
    5 4
+   6 2
_____

_____
```

4.
```
  H T U
    3 6
    4 9
    7 2
    3 4
+   1 8
_____

_____
```

5.
```
  H T U
    4 8
    2 8
    3 9
    4 6
+   5 9
_____

_____
```

> Use a number grid.

> Choose 3 touching numbers in a straight line.

> Add them.

> Write 10 additions.

> How close to 100 can you get?

Number grid
(1 to 100)

1	2	3	4	5	6	7	8	9	10
11	12	13	14	15	16	17	18	19	20
21	22	23	24	25	26	27	28	29	30
31	32	33	34	35	36	37	38	39	40
41	42	43	44	45	46	47	48	49	50
51	52	53	54	55	56	57	58	59	60
61	62	63	64	65	66	67	68	69	70
71	72	73	74	75	76	77	78	79	80
81	82	83	84	85	86	87	88	89	90
91	92	93	94	95	96	97	98	99	100

Threes

Copy and complete.

$1 \times 3 =$

$1 \times 3 = 3$

$2 \times 3 = 6$

$3 \times 3 =$

$4 \times 3 =$

$5 \times 3 = 15$

$6 \times 3 =$

$7 \times 3 =$

$8 \times 3 =$

$9 \times 3 =$

$10 \times 3 =$

Explore

Add the digits of your answers above.
What do you notice?

$\underline{1\,2}$ $1 + 2 = 3$

Write the missing numbers.

1. 3, 6, 9, 12,

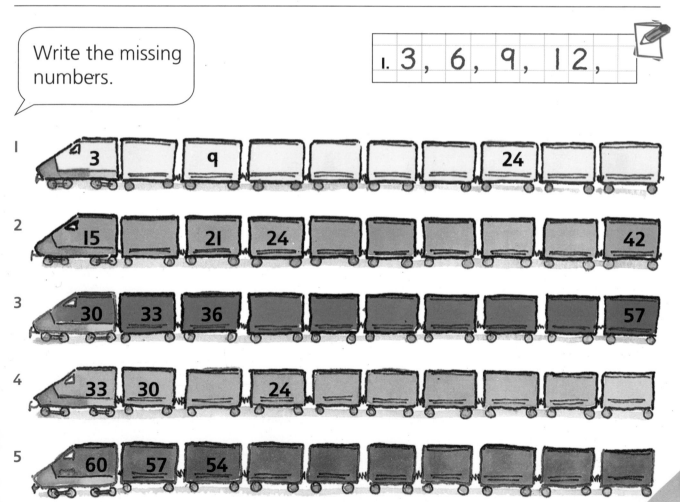

1 3 ___ 9 ___ ___ ___ ___ 24 ___ ___

2 15 ___ 21 24 ___ ___ ___ ___ ___ 42

3 30 33 36 ___ ___ ___ ___ ___ ___ 57

4 33 30 ___ 24 ___ ___ ___ ___ ___ ___

5 60 57 54 ___ ___ ___ ___ ___ ___ ___

Copy and complete.

$1 \times 4 =$

$1 \times 4 = 4$

$2 \times 4 =$ $3 \times 4 =$ $4 \times 4 =$

$5 \times 4 =$ $6 \times 4 =$ $7 \times 4 =$

$8 \times 4 =$ $9 \times 4 =$ $10 \times 4 =$

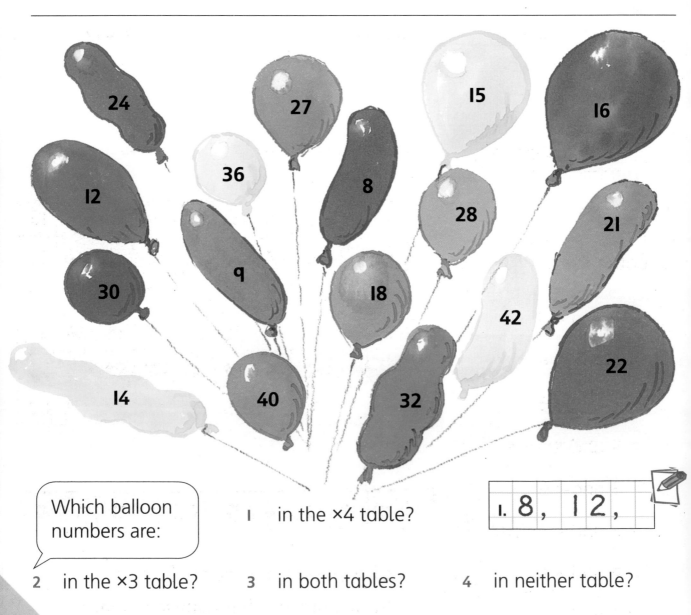

Which balloon numbers are:

1 in the ×4 table?

1. 8, 12,

2 in the ×3 table? 3 in both tables? 4 in neither table?

Threes and fours

Copy and complete.

1 ⬤ × 4 = 16

    1. $4 \times 4 = 16$

2 ⬤ × 3 = 18

3 5 × 4 = ⬤

4 7 × ⬤ = 21

5 ⬤ × 4 = 32

6 ⬤ × 3 = 27

7 ⬤ × 4 = 28

8 8 × ⬤ = 24

9 9 × 4 = ⬤

10 ⬤ × 3 = 12

Explore

Write grid
numbers that are
in both tables.

1	2	3	4	5	6	7	8	9	10
11	12	13	14	15	16	17	18	19	20
21	22	23	24	25	26	27	28	29	30
31	32	33	34	35	36	37	38	39	40
41	42	43	44	45	46	47	48	49	50
51	52	53	54	55	56	57	58	59	60

11 × 2 and × 3

12 × 3 and × 4

13 × 3 and × 5

14 × 4 and × 5

15 × 3 and × 10

16 × 2 and × 5

17 × 4 and × 10

18 × 2 and × 4

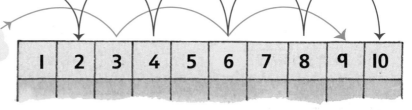

×2

×3

1	2	3	4	5	6	7	8	9	10

Choose your own pairs of tables.

Write numbers that appear in both.

Copy and complete.

1 × 8 =

$1 \times 8 = 8$

2 × 8 =

3 × 8 =

4 × 8 =

5 × 8 =

6 × 8 =

7 × 8 =

8 × 8 =

9 × 8 =

10 × 8 =

Each spider has 8 legs.

How many legs in each group?

1. $3 \times 8 = 24$

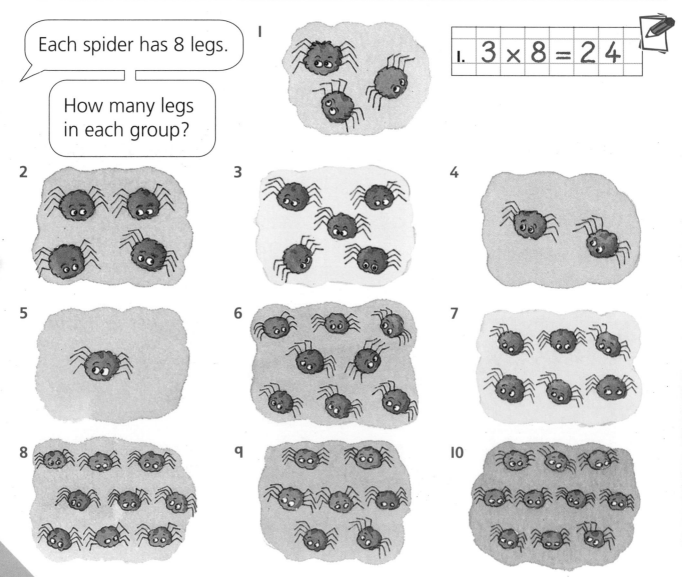

Fours and eights

Copy and complete.

1. $2 \times 4 = 8, \; 2 \times 8 = 16$

1	$2 \times 4 =$	$2 \times 8 =$
2	$3 \times 4 =$	$3 \times 8 =$
3	$4 \times 4 =$	$4 \times 8 =$
4	$5 \times 4 =$	$5 \times 8 =$
5	$6 \times 4 =$	$6 \times 8 =$
6	$7 \times 4 =$	$7 \times 8 =$

To find the second answer on each line, double the first answer.

Each sticker costs 8p.

How much does each set cost?

7. $3 \times 8p = 24p$

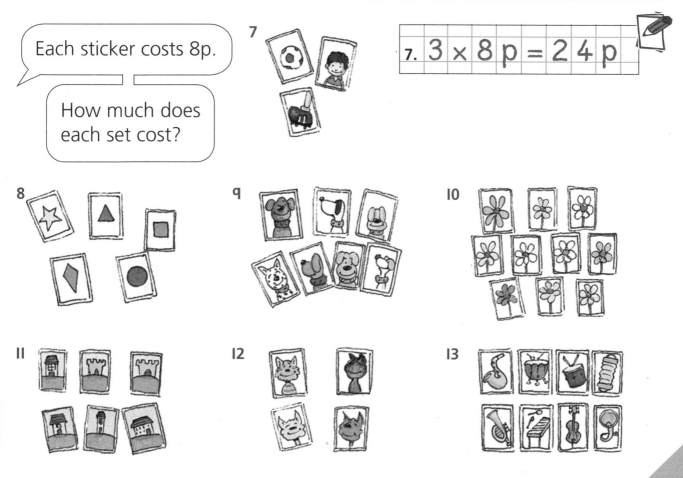

Which boat numbers are:

1 in the ×4 table?

	8	,	12	,	

2 in the ×8 table?   3 in both tables?   4 in neither table?

At Home

Make ten cards, numbered I to 10, out of an old greetings card. Shuffle them and place them face down in a pile.

Take turns to turn over a card and spin a coin.

Score 8 for 'heads' and 4 for 'tails'.

Multiply the card number by your score, and keep a running total.

The winner is the first to reach over 200.

Fours and eights

Double each answer.

Write it in eights (×8).

1. double 4 0 = 8 0
   1 0 × 8 = 8 0

1 10 × 4 = 40

2 6 × 4 = 24

3 13 × 4 = 52

4 15 × 4 = 60

5 8 × 4 = 32

6 12 × 4 = 48

7 20 × 4 = 80

8 11 × 4 = 44

9 100 × 4 = 400

10 9 × 4 = 36

Explore

These numbers are in the ×4 table.

4   8   12   16   20   24   28   32   36   40

These are their units digits: 4, 8, 2, 6, …

Write more numbers in the ×4 table and look for a pattern.

Do the same for numbers in the ×8 table.

Nines

Copy and complete.

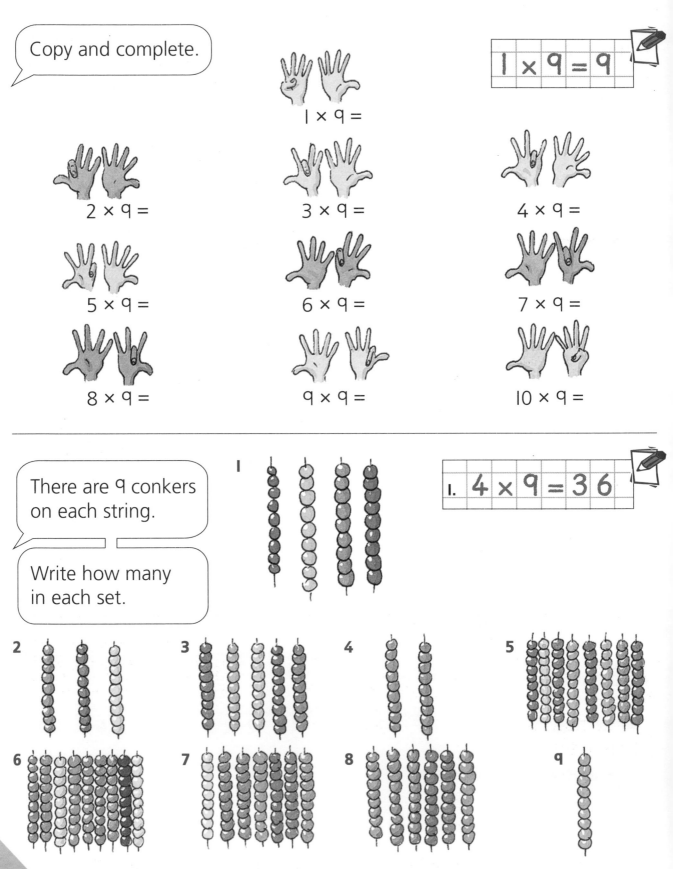

$1 \times 9 =$

$1 \times 9 = 9$

$2 \times 9 =$

$3 \times 9 =$

$4 \times 9 =$

$5 \times 9 =$

$6 \times 9 =$

$7 \times 9 =$

$8 \times 9 =$

$9 \times 9 =$

$10 \times 9 =$

There are 9 conkers on each string.

Write how many in each set.

1

1. $4 \times 9 = 36$

2

3

4

5

6

7

8

9

38

Nines

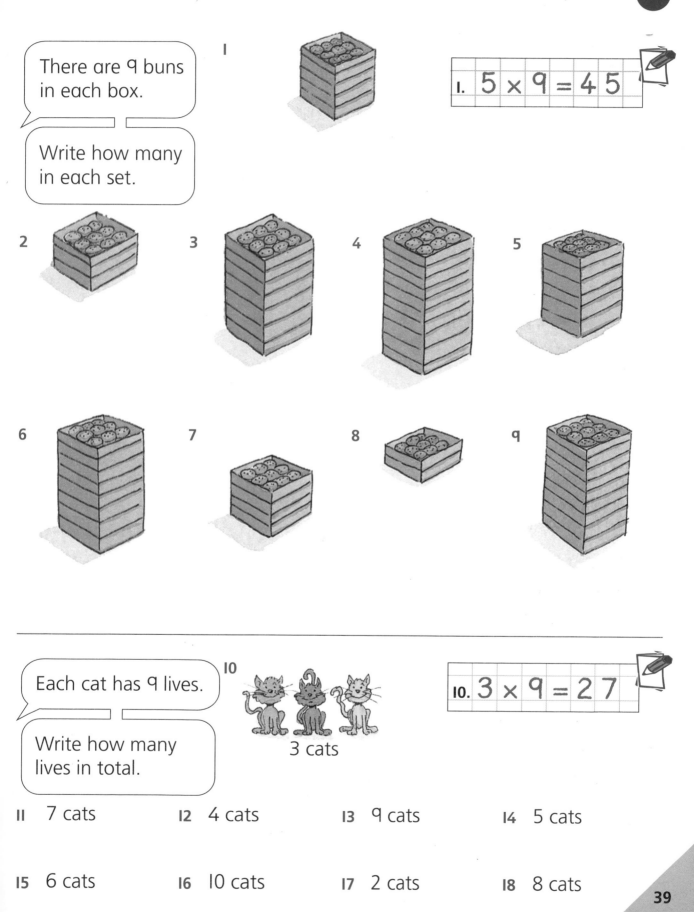

There are 9 buns in each box.

Write how many in each set.

1. $5 \times 9 = 45$

2

3

4

5

6

7

8

9

Each cat has 9 lives.

Write how many lives in total.

3 cats

10. $3 \times 9 = 27$

| 11 | 7 cats | 12 | 4 cats | 13 | 9 cats | 14 | 5 cats |
| 15 | 6 cats | 16 | 10 cats | 17 | 2 cats | 18 | 8 cats |

Nines

> Each blast is worth 9 points. Write the totals.

1. $5 \times 9 = 45$

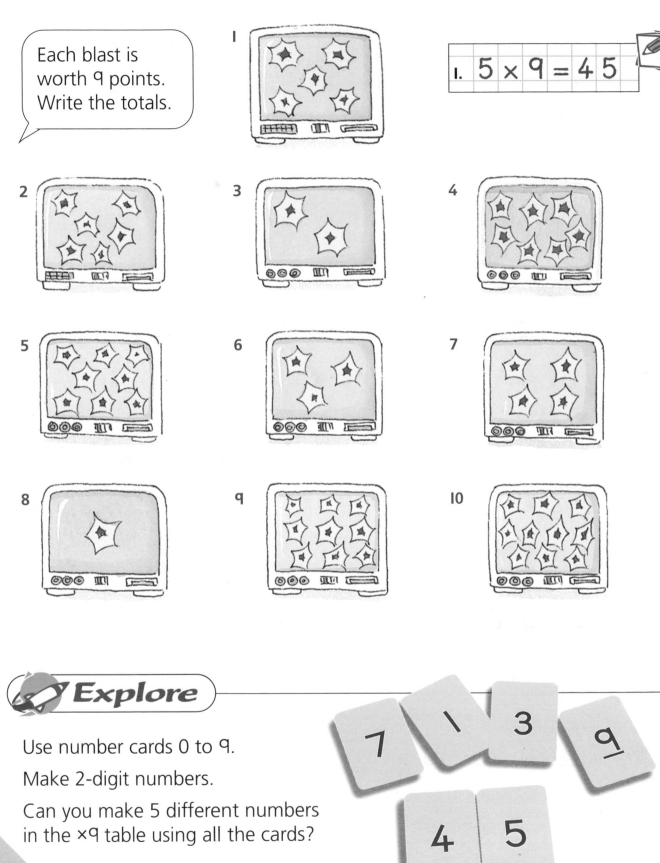

Explore

Use number cards 0 to 9.

Make 2-digit numbers.

Can you make 5 different numbers in the ×9 table using all the cards?

7 1 3 9

4 5

40

Pattern in nines

Write a multiplication for each star number.

1. $1 \times 9 = 9$

1	2	3	4	5	6	7	8	9	10
11	12	13	14	15	16	17	18	19	20
21	22	23	24	25	26	27	28	29	30
31	32	33	34	35	36	37	38	39	40
41	42	43	44	45	46	47	48	49	50
51	52	53	54	55	56	57	58	59	60
61	62	63	64	65	66	67	68	69	70
71	72	73	74	75	76	77	78	79	80
81	82	83	84	85	86	87	88	89	90
91	92	93	94	95	96	97	98	99	100

Explore

Here are the first numbers in the ×3 table.

3, 6, 9, 12, …

Copy and continue up to 60.

Circle any numbers in the ×9 table.

What do you notice about nines and threes?

Pattern in nines

Copy and complete.

I. $2 \times 9 = 18$, $1 + 8 = 9$

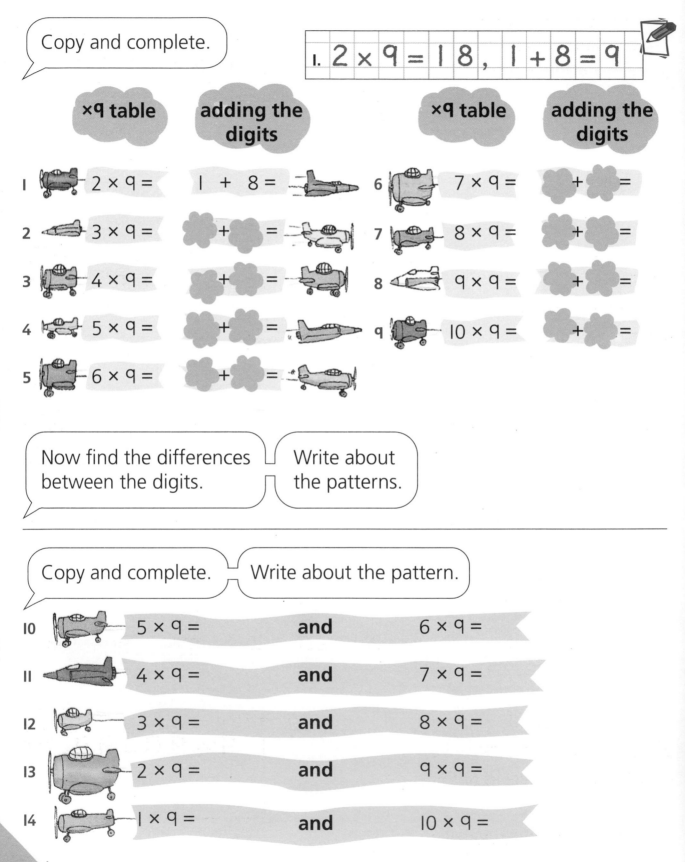

×9 table   **adding the digits**   **×9 table**   **adding the digits**

1. $2 \times 9 =$ $1 + 8 =$ 6. $7 \times 9 =$ $+ =$

2. $3 \times 9 =$ $+ =$ 7. $8 \times 9 =$ $+ =$

3. $4 \times 9 =$ $+ =$ 8. $9 \times 9 =$ $+ =$

4. $5 \times 9 =$ $+ =$ 9. $10 \times 9 =$ $+ =$

5. $6 \times 9 =$ $+ =$

Now find the differences between the digits.

Write about the patterns.

Copy and complete. — Write about the pattern.

10. $5 \times 9 =$ **and** $6 \times 9 =$

11. $4 \times 9 =$ **and** $7 \times 9 =$

12. $3 \times 9 =$ **and** $8 \times 9 =$

13. $2 \times 9 =$ **and** $9 \times 9 =$

14. $1 \times 9 =$ **and** $10 \times 9 =$

Pattern in nines

Copy and complete.

1 9 × 9 =

| 1. | 9 | × | 9 | = | 8 | 1 |

2 11 × 9 =   3 8 × 9 =   4 13 × 9 =

5 7 × 9 =   6 12 × 9 =   7 10 × 9 =

Which of these are in the ×9 table?

| | 9 | 9 | , | |

18

19

81   56   108   89   99   119   90   45

Here are the nines.

9   18   27   36   45   54   63   72   81   90

Add the first and last.

Add the next pair. Continue.

Write about the pattern.

| 9 | + | 9 | 0 | = | 9 | 9 |
| 1 | 8 | + | 8 | 1 | = | |

Copy and complete.

1. $10 - 1 = 9$

Number grid
(1 to 100)

1   $10 - 1 =$

2   $20 - 2 =$

3   $30 - 3 =$

4   $40 - 4 =$

5   $50 - 5 =$

6   $60 - 6 =$

7   $70 - 7 =$

8   $80 - 8 =$

9   $90 - 9 =$

10   $100 - 10 =$

1	2	3	4	5	6	7	8	9	10
11	12	13	14	15	16	17	18	19	20
21	22	23	24	25	26	27	28	29	30
31	32	33	34	35	36	37	38	39	40
41	42	43	44	45	46	47	48	49	50
51	52	53	54	55	56	57	58	59	60
61	62	63	64	65	66	67	68	69	70
71	72	73	74	75	76	77	78	79	80
81	82	83	84	85	86	87	88	89	90
91	92	93	94	95	96	97	98	99	100

Colour the tens on your grid.

Colour the nines a different colour.

At Home

Make ten cards with numbers from the ×9 table.

Shuffle them and place them face down.

Take turns to choose a card and say the matching number of nines.

If you are wrong replace the card.

Continue until all the cards are gone.

90   63   54   27   18   72   36   9   45   81

Fractions

Copy each grid and colour the fraction shown.

1    $\frac{1}{4}$

I. $\frac{1}{4}$

2    $\frac{1}{3}$

3    $\frac{1}{4}$

4    $\frac{1}{6}$

5    $\frac{1}{3}$

6    $\frac{1}{2}$

7    $\frac{1}{8}$

8    $\frac{1}{4}$

9    $\frac{1}{5}$

10    $\frac{1}{2}$

What fraction of each set is red?

11

II. $\frac{1}{4}$

12

13

14

15

16

17

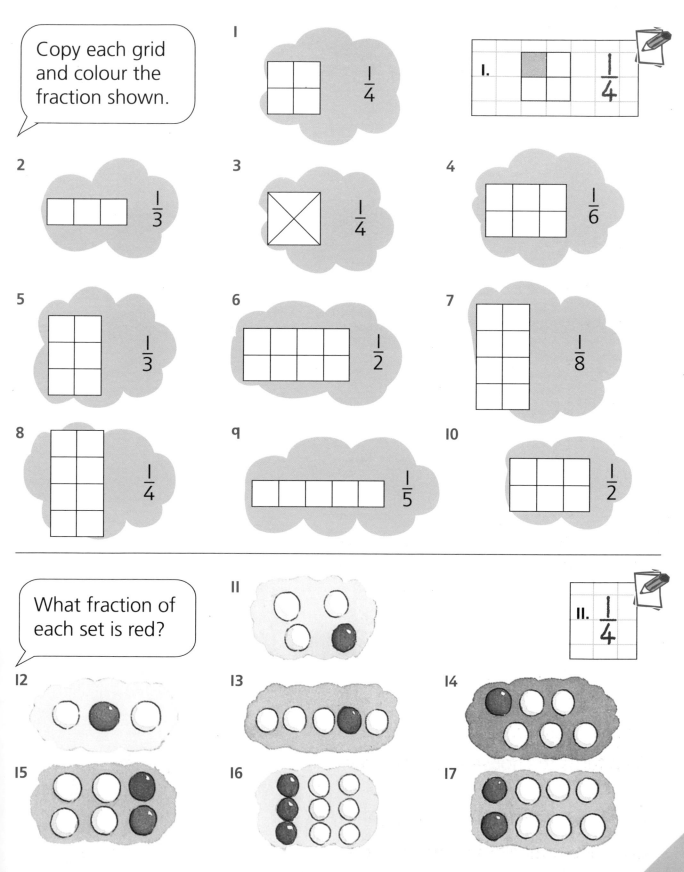

45

Fractions

Write the fraction
of each shape
that is blue.

I. $\dfrac{3}{4}$

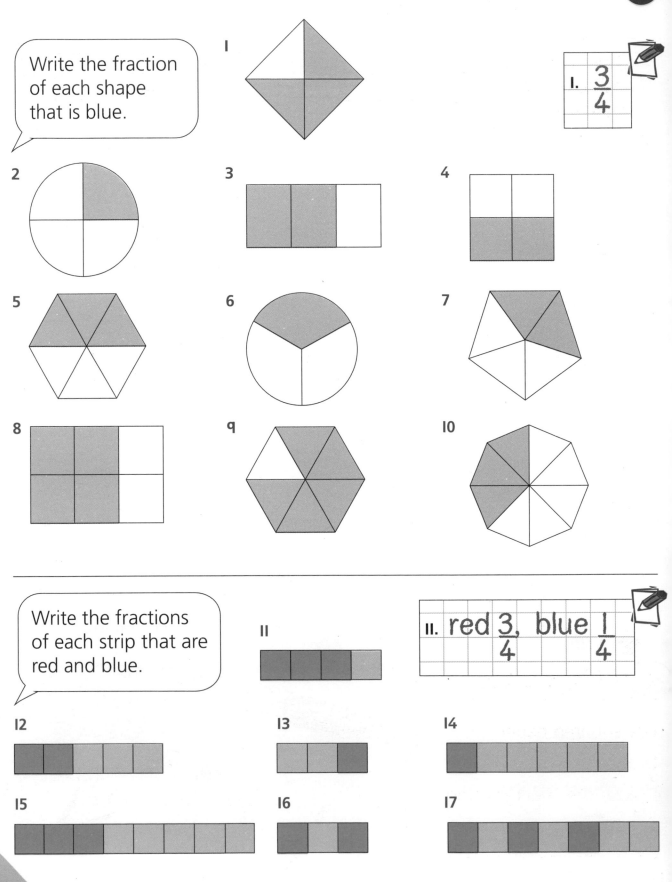

Write the fractions
of each strip that are
red and blue.

II. red $\dfrac{3}{4}$, blue $\dfrac{1}{4}$

Fractions

Copy each grid and colour the fraction shown.

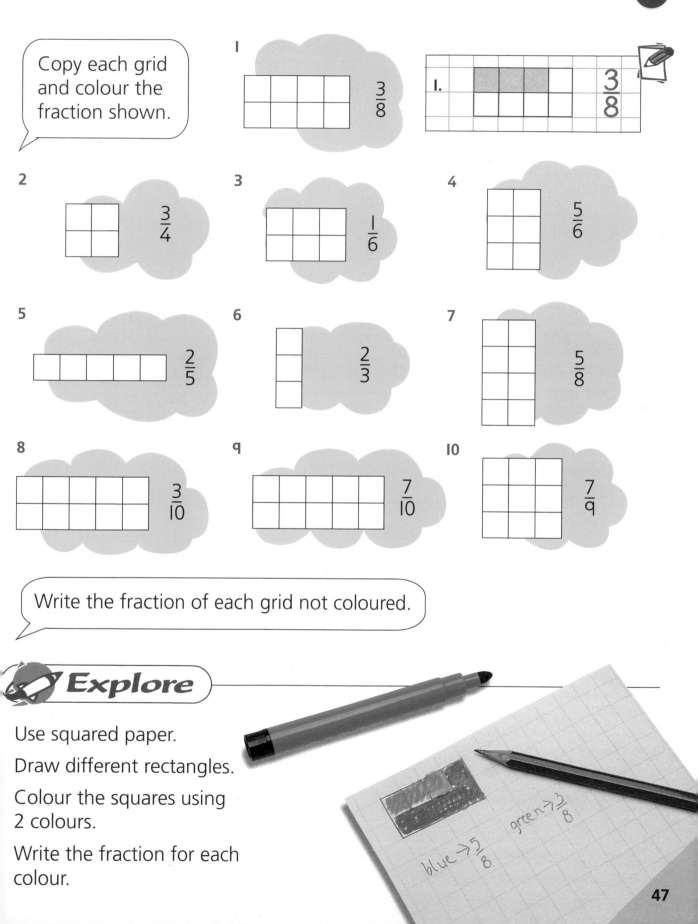

1    $\frac{3}{8}$

I. $\frac{3}{8}$

2    $\frac{3}{4}$

3    $\frac{1}{6}$

4    $\frac{5}{6}$

5    $\frac{2}{5}$

6    $\frac{2}{3}$

7    $\frac{5}{8}$

8    $\frac{3}{10}$

9    $\frac{7}{10}$

10    $\frac{7}{9}$

Write the fraction of each grid not coloured.

Explore

Use squared paper.

Draw different rectangles.

Colour the squares using 2 colours.

Write the fraction for each colour.

blue → $\frac{5}{8}$ green → $\frac{3}{8}$

Fractions

Draw different strips and colour these fractions.

1 $\frac{2}{5}$

1. 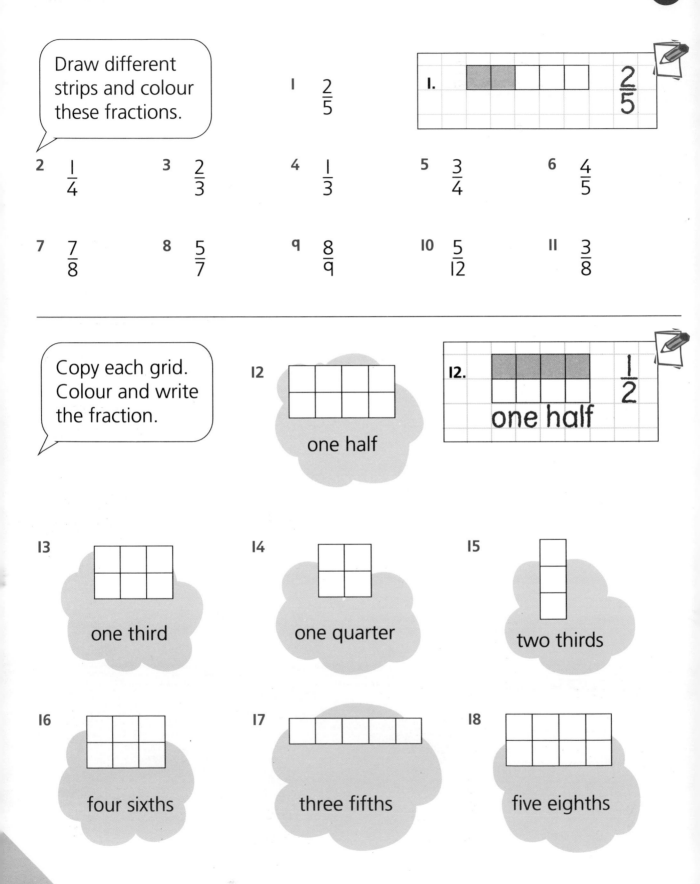 $\frac{2}{5}$

2 $\frac{1}{4}$

3 $\frac{2}{3}$

4 $\frac{1}{3}$

5 $\frac{3}{4}$

6 $\frac{4}{5}$

7 $\frac{7}{8}$

8 $\frac{5}{7}$

9 $\frac{8}{9}$

10 $\frac{5}{12}$

11 $\frac{3}{8}$

Copy each grid. Colour and write the fraction.

12 one half

12. one half $\frac{1}{2}$

13 one third

14 one quarter

15 two thirds

16 four sixths

17 three fifths

18 five eighths

48

Fractions

Write what fraction of these are:

1. red

I. $\dfrac{3}{10}$

2. buses
3. lorries
4. cars
5. blue
6. yellow
7. orange
8. blue lorries
9. not cars

Write what fraction of these.

10. are black
11. are happy
12. are ginger
13. have 4 whiskers
14. are sad
15. are white
16. are grey

Matching fractions

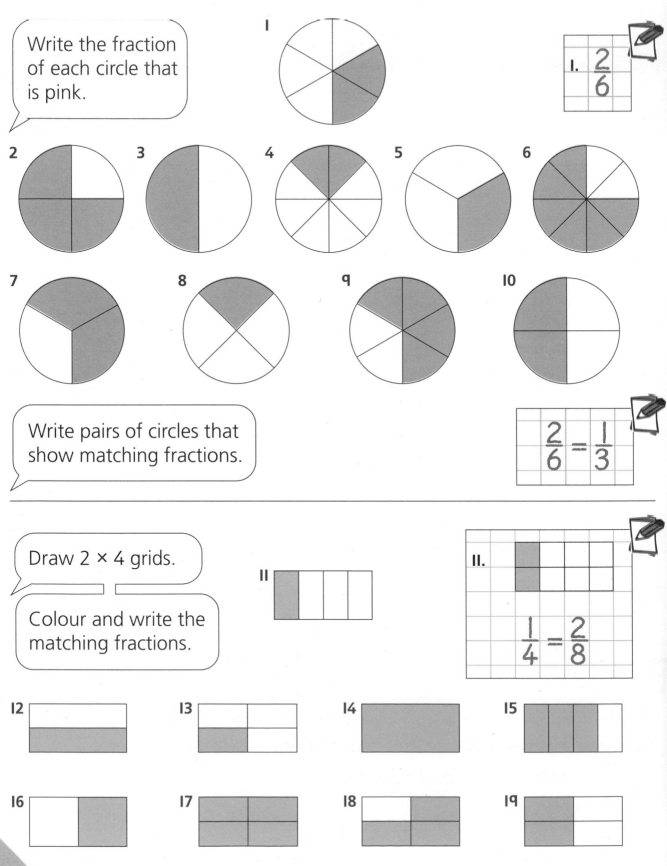

Write the fraction of each circle that is pink.

I. $\dfrac{2}{6}$

Write pairs of circles that show matching fractions.

$\dfrac{2}{6} = \dfrac{1}{3}$

Draw 2 × 4 grids.

Colour and write the matching fractions.

II. $\dfrac{1}{4} = \dfrac{2}{8}$

Matching fractions

Write pairs of fractions that match.

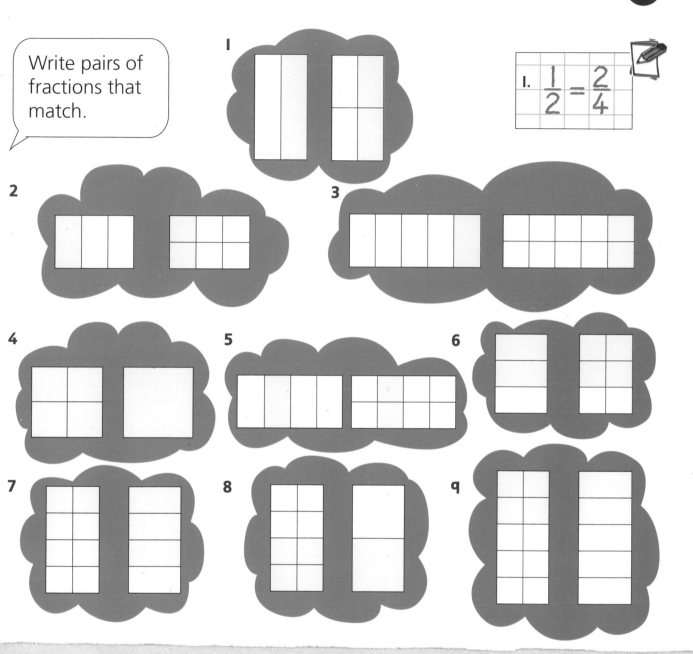

1. $\frac{1}{2} = \frac{2}{4}$

At Home

Write a fraction, hidden from your partner, and read it aloud.

Your partner must write a matching fraction.

Check that they match by drawing and colouring grids.

Take three turns each. Bring all your fraction pairs in to school.

Matching fractions

> Write missing numbers to make the pairs of fractions match.

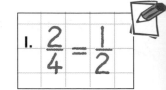

I. $\dfrac{2}{4} = \dfrac{1}{2}$

1
$$\dfrac{}{4} = \dfrac{1}{2}$$

2
$$\dfrac{}{8} = \dfrac{1}{4}$$

3
$$\dfrac{}{2} = \text{I whole}$$

4
$$\dfrac{}{8} = \dfrac{2}{4}$$

5
$$\dfrac{}{8} = \dfrac{1}{2}$$

6
$$\dfrac{}{4} = \text{I whole}$$

7
$$\dfrac{}{8} = \dfrac{3}{4}$$

8
$$\dfrac{}{8} = \text{I whole}$$

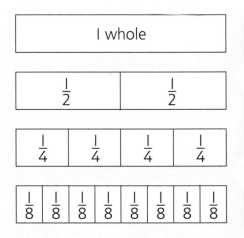

> Write missing numbers to make the pairs of fractions match.

9
$$\dfrac{}{6} = \dfrac{1}{3}$$

10
$$\dfrac{}{2} = \text{I whole}$$

11
$$\dfrac{}{6} = \dfrac{1}{2}$$

12
$$\dfrac{}{3} = \text{I whole}$$

13
$$\dfrac{}{6} = \text{I whole}$$

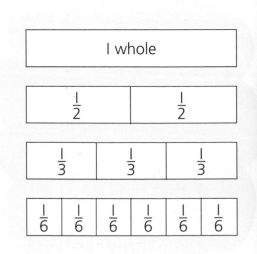

Fractions

Copy and complete.

1. $\frac{1}{4}$ of 12p = 3p

1 $\frac{1}{4}$ of 12p =

2 $\frac{2}{4}$ of 12p =

3 $\frac{3}{4}$ of 12p =

4 $\frac{4}{4}$ of 12p =

5 $\frac{1}{3}$ of 15p =

6 $\frac{2}{3}$ of 15p =

7 $\frac{3}{3}$ of 15p =

8 $\frac{1}{5}$ of 20p =

9 $\frac{2}{5}$ of 20p =

10 $\frac{3}{5}$ of 20p =

11 $\frac{4}{5}$ of 20p =

12 $\frac{5}{5}$ of 20p =

Explore

Use 10p coins.

Make equal piles.

Write different fractions.

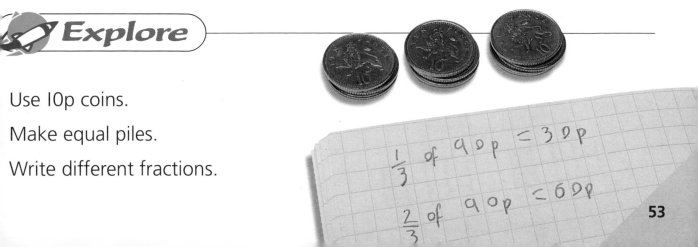

$\frac{1}{3}$ of 90p = 30p

$\frac{2}{3}$ of 90p = 60p

53

Fractions

> Write this fraction of each set.

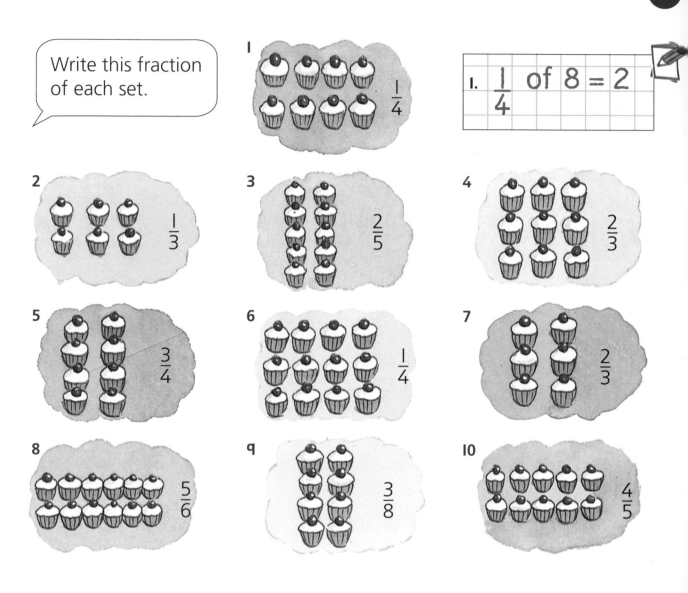

1. $\frac{1}{4}$

I. $\frac{1}{4}$ of $8 = 2$

2. $\frac{1}{3}$

3. $\frac{2}{5}$

4. $\frac{2}{3}$

5. $\frac{3}{4}$

6. $\frac{1}{4}$

7. $\frac{2}{3}$

8. $\frac{5}{6}$

9. $\frac{3}{8}$

10. $\frac{4}{5}$

> Copy and complete.

11. $\frac{1}{3}$ of $9 =$

II. $\frac{1}{3}$ of $9 = 3$

12. $\frac{1}{4}$ of $8 =$

13. $\frac{2}{4}$ of $8 =$

14. $\frac{3}{4}$ of $8 =$

15. $\frac{1}{3}$ of $6 =$

16. $\frac{2}{3}$ of $6 =$

17. $\frac{3}{3}$ of $6 =$

> Use counters to help you.

18. $\frac{1}{2}$ of $12 =$

Fractions

> Write the fraction of each set that is red.

1

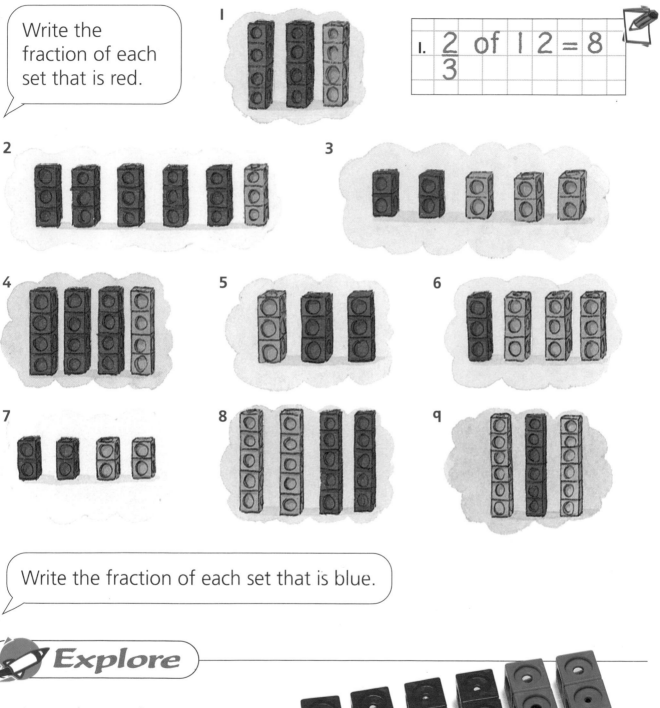

I. $\dfrac{2}{3}$ of 12 = 8

2

3

4

5

6

7

8

9

> Write the fraction of each set that is blue.

Explore

Using only 12 cubes, make a set of red and blue towers (each tower must be the same height).

Draw the towers and write the fraction of red cubes and blue cubes.

red → $\dfrac{4}{6}$ blue → $\dfrac{2}{6}$

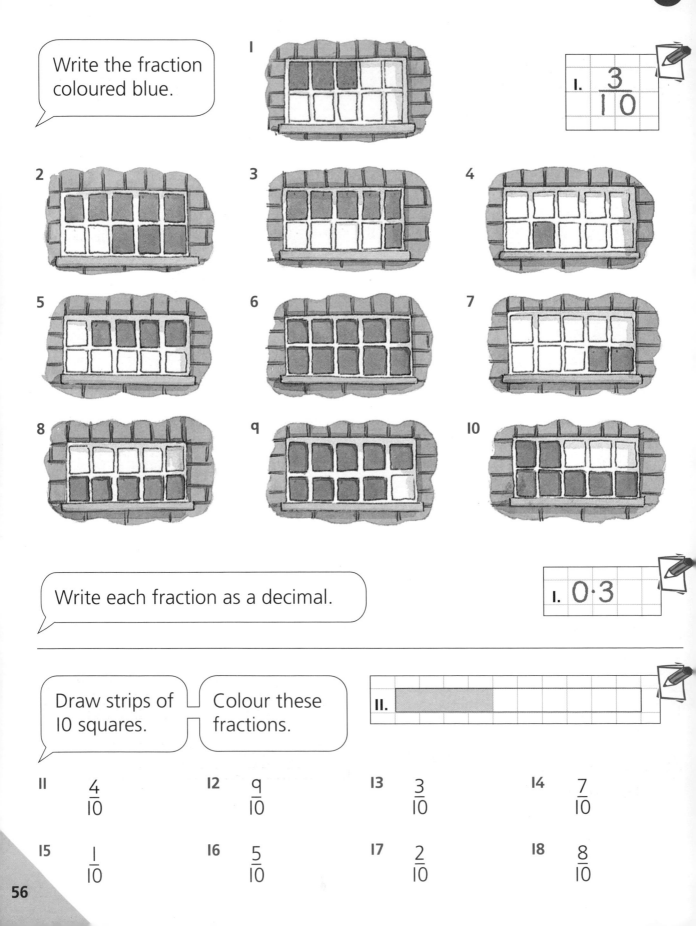

Write the fraction coloured blue.

I. $\frac{3}{10}$

Write each fraction as a decimal.

I. 0·3

Draw strips of 10 squares. Colour these fractions.

II.

11 $\frac{4}{10}$

12 $\frac{9}{10}$

13 $\frac{3}{10}$

14 $\frac{7}{10}$

15 $\frac{1}{10}$

16 $\frac{5}{10}$

17 $\frac{2}{10}$

18 $\frac{8}{10}$

Tenths

Write the fraction coloured red.

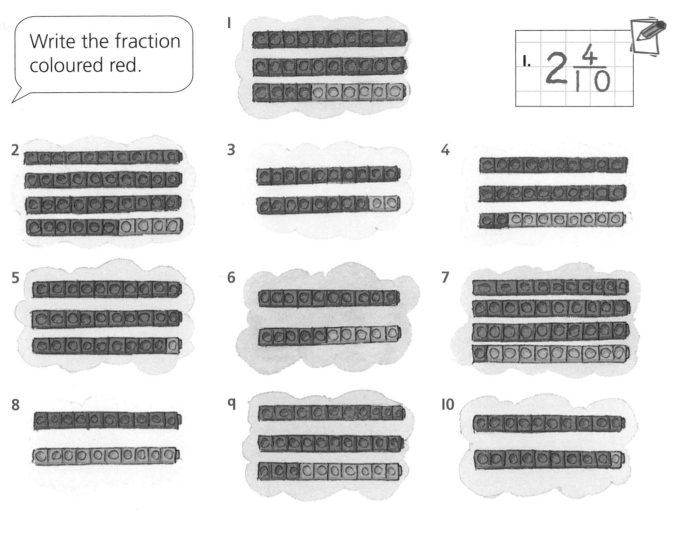

I. $2\frac{4}{10}$

Write each fraction above as a decimal.

I. 2·4

Draw strips of 10 squares.

Colour these fractions.

11   1·6

12   2·3

13   1·8   14   1·3   15   1·1   16   2·9

17   1·5   18   1·4   19   2·1   20   1·7

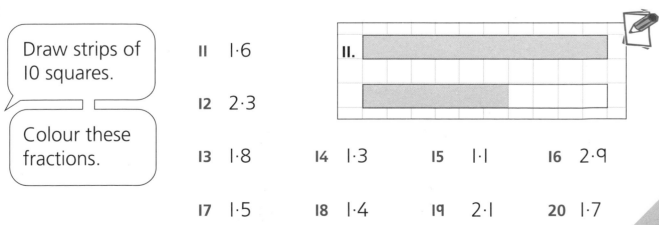

II.

57

Write the balloon numbers in order from smallest to largest.

Colour strips of 10 to help you.

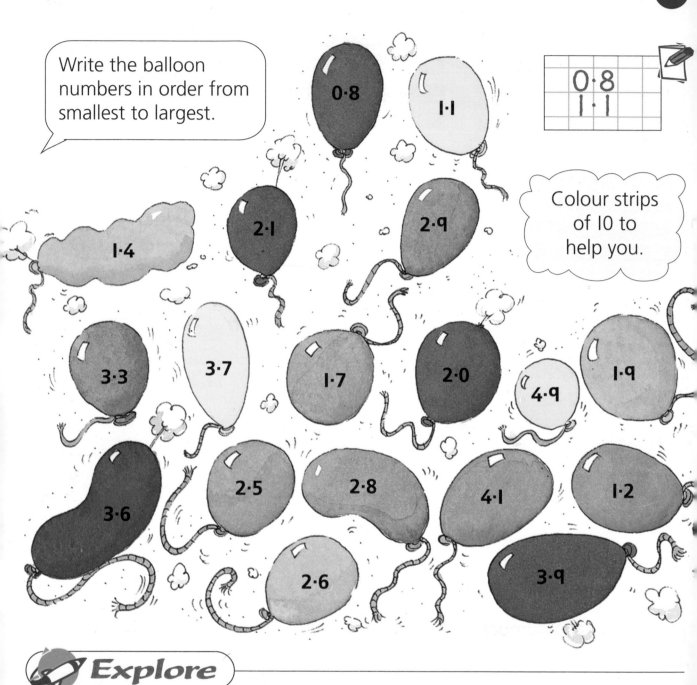

0·8
1·1
1·4
2·1
2·9
3·3
3·7
1·7
2·0
4·9
1·9
3·6
2·5
2·8
4·1
1·2
2·6
3·9

0·8
1·1

Explore

Draw some strips 10 squares long.

Split them into 3 parts using 3 colours. Write matching fractions.

Explore different ways of splitting the strips.

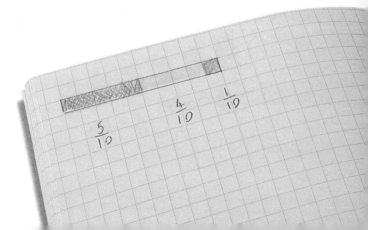

$\frac{5}{10}$ $\frac{4}{10}$ $\frac{1}{10}$

Tenths

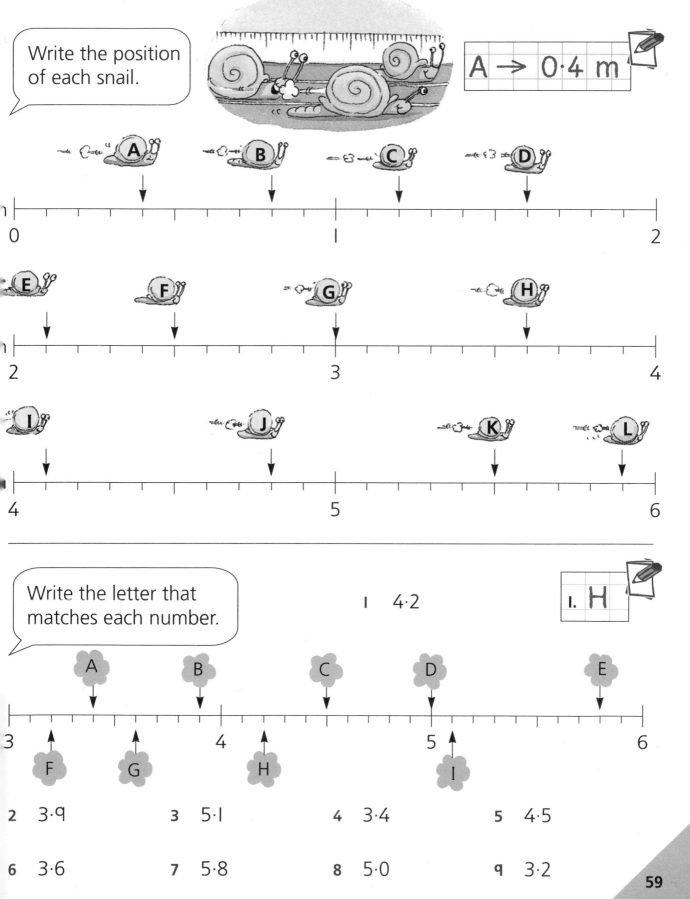

Tenths

Write each weight.

1.   2·4 kg

2.

3.

4.

5.

6.

7.

8.   0·5 ,   0·6 ,   0·7

Write the hidden numbers.

8   0·2 0·3 0·4   0·8 0·9 1·0

9   0·9 1·0 1·1   1·5 1·6

10   2·1 2·2 2·3   2·7 2·8

11   0·8 0·9   1·4 1·5

12   0·5 0·6   1·1 1·2

13   1·8 1·9 2·0   2·6 2·7

Tenths

Write these weights in order from smallest to largest.

1·1 kg

| 1·1 kg |
| 1·2 kg |

2·4 kg

3·1 kg

3·4 kg

2·9 kg

1·2 kg

4·5 kg

2·8 kg

5·5 kg

3·9 kg

4·1 kg

5·0 kg

Explore

Use number cards 2, 3, 5.

Use 2 cards to make different decimal numbers.

How many can you make?

Write them in order from smallest to largest.

5   3   2

2·3
2·5

Copy and complete.

$1 \times 10 =$

$1 \times 10 = 10$

$2 \times 10 =$ $3 \times 10 =$ $4 \times 10 =$

$5 \times 10 =$ $6 \times 10 =$ $7 \times 10 =$

$8 \times 10 =$ $9 \times 10 =$ $10 \times 10 =$

$13 \times 10 =$ $16 \times 10 =$ $18 \times 10 =$

$11 \times 10 =$ $17 \times 10 =$ $20 \times 10 =$

Each squid has 10 legs.

How many legs in each group?

$1. \ 4 \times 10 = 40$

Each apple costs 10p.

How much does each group cost?

1. $13 \times 10p = 130p$

1 **13 apples**

2 **19 apples**

3 **23 apples**

4 **10 apples**

5 **21 apples**

6 **30 apples**

7 **22 apples**

8 **16 apples**

9 **15 apples**

10 **5 apples**

How many apples can you buy with these amounts?

11 350p

11. **35 apples**

12 480p   13 10p   14 100p   15 280p   16 560p

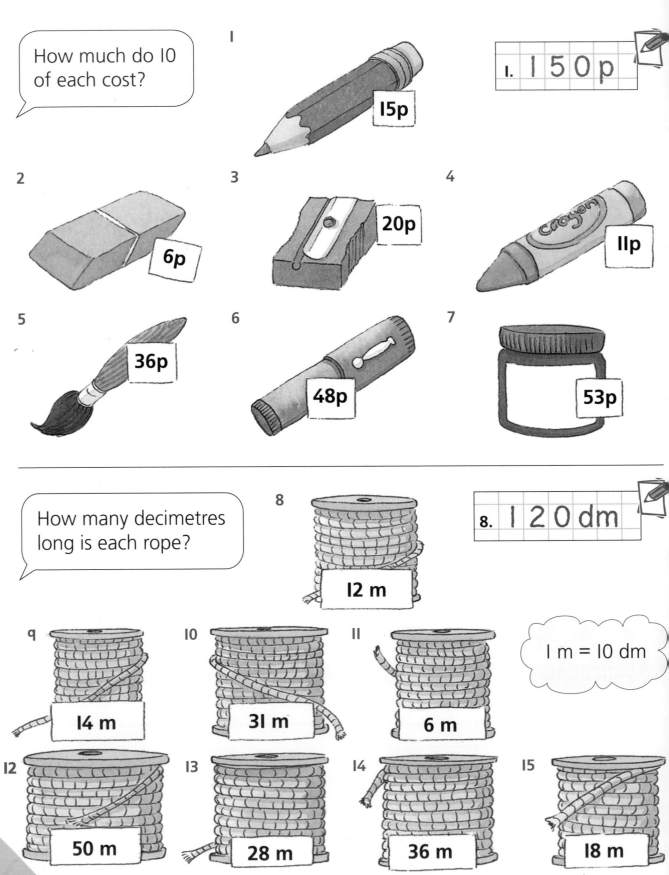

How much do 10 of each cost?

1
15p

1. 150p

2
6p

3
20p

4
llp

5
36p

6
48p

7
53p

How many decimetres long is each rope?

8
12 m

8. 120 dm

9
14 m

10
31 m

11
6 m

1 m = 10 dm

12
50 m

13
28 m

14
36 m

15
18 m